HOLZ books 2018

SPACE ADVENTURES

coloring book

GALAXY
NEWS

WELCOME
TO
SPACE

SPACE
ADVENTURES

www.ingramcontent.com/pod-product-compliance
Lightning Source LLC
Chambersburg PA
CBHW081653220526
45468CB00009B/2636
* 9 7 8 1 7 9 2 7 2 8 5 9 4 *